This book is dedicated to God who created a universe in which we can be successful in.

Table of Contents

INTRODUCTION

First, I want to say thank you for purchasing this book. I had a ton of fun creating and writing this book for the sole purpose that it will help people like you live a better life. Being financially free has personally helped me be a better husband, father, and overall person. My personal thanks goes to my wife Johana for always being supportive on my endeavors in life along with being an amazing mother of my children.

My goal in writing this book is to help as many people achieve the same, if not better, success than me.

Through this short book you will learn some of the most valuable lessons you can learn, like how to secure financial freedom and unlock a better life for you and your family. I encourage you to keep an open mind and think deep about each subject that is talked about. I have done my best to explain everything in simple terms to help make the lessons easy to learn. In this book I have included a lot of my job history starting all the way back to when I was 10 years old. I felt it was necessary to include this, so that you have a better understanding of where some of these key lessons have come from in my journey to financial freedom. Some of you may relate to some of the struggles I had to overcome. I hope this encourages you to see how financial freedom can be accomplished with the right mindset and drive. I look forward to hearing more success stories from individuals that have eliminated the excuses and have taken action to enhance their lives!

Before you continue forward, I want to explain the difference between expenses and assets. These terms will be used frequently to give you direction on what your next steps are to financial freedom.

Expenses in the simplest of definitions are items that cost you money every month. Such as a car, boat or a weekend getaway.

Assets are items you own that make you money every month, such as a real estate rental property, or a business. Keep in mind the difference between the two as you read on.

CHAPTER ONE

Who am I?

To tell you a little about myself, I live in a great neighborhood in sunny Southern California. I have an amazing wife and four beautiful kids. Two boys and two girls. They are the absolute joy of my life and the reason why I wanted to become financially free.

At a young age, I was a go getter to say the least. When I was 10 years old I got my first job. I played a beautiful white baby grand piano at the local grocery store during the Christmas holiday season. I realized at a young age the things I wanted in life cost money, therefore I must make a ton of it due to my desire for nice things. I was making $10 an hour and about $20 an hour in tips. $30 an hour at 10 years old was not bad at all right? Well, after I bought my favorite toys the money quickly disappeared! After Christmas the local grocery store would put the white baby grand piano back into storage and poof, there went my income. I realized if I want to keep buying my favorite things I needed to find a way to make money year round.

Next, I started to sell oranges, avocados, licorice, and airhead candies door to door and to other students in school for a profit. I saved up enough money to pay for a brand new dirt bike! I was a very happy camper that day and promised myself I would keep working hard so I can get anything I want in life.

Fast forward a few years later when I was 14, my grandparents owned a series of apartment complexes in California, so I asked if I could work for them by cleaning up the properties after school. They gladly accepted the offer and I continued to do that work until around 16 years old. As I cleaned the hallways and picked up trash two times a week, I quickly became fascinated with the idea of owning rental property. The idea of providing a clean safe environment for families to live in, and receive rental income, became a burning desire as time went on. At the time I didn't know it, but this desire would fuel an empire later in life.

When I was 16 I also started working at that same grocery store where I played the piano, but in a different position. I was the friendly neighborhood bag boy. I worked there for two years and the day I turned 18 they promoted me to work in the meat department. Around this same time I started working a second job at night which was a full time construction gig down in San Diego, CA. Two jobs at 18 years old took away a lot of "hanging out with friends" time, however I had a feeling it would pay big dividends somewhere down the line. Eventually the construction job started paying much more than the grocery store, so I willfully left the grocery job and focused on construction. Unfortunately, after about 3 months the construction company hit a bad run and eventually went belly up. This put me completely out of work and therefore out of income.

So there I was now jobless again but had all the ambition in the world to make money. I just needed a clear path to do so. I thought to myself, what industry can I work in and not have the business go belly up? Sales jobs were the first thing that came to mind. Companies will always need someone to sell their products. It felt like a good path to travel down. I then pursued a job in sales. I got my license to sell insurance and hit the ground running! I made it a point to learn something new every day and never have an issue with any amount of work it would take to be successful. My goal was to break records and dominate my field. As time went on, I rose up the ranks from Trainee, to Agent, to Assistant Manager, to Branch Manager, to District Manager then to Vice President. I don't want to bore you with the details of all the hard work and dedication that went into proving myself for each rank but trust me, it was no easy task! Plus, the purpose of this book as you will read later is to focus on building assets, and a job is not an asset.

As my income went up I made the same mistake most people make by raising my expenses. New Rank = Higher Pay = Nicer Car/House. I realized that I will never be financially free if I continue to build my expenses and not focus on building my asset income. So, when I was 25 I decided to TAKE ACTION!

I made a commitment to myself to learn how to build financial wealth from as many people who have achieved it as possible. Some mentors were great and easy to learn from and some were tough and told it the straight forward way. Still to this day I am appreciative of all of them and will gladly help each of them whenever they need it. So, what did I do to take action at the age of 25? Well, aside from making the commitment of never using an excuse to stop me from achieving my goal, I asked myself, "What am I passionate about"? I quickly had a flashback to when I was just 14 years old working at my grandparent's apartment complexes. I remembered how awesome it would be to own a huge property that provides great living conditions for so many families. I decided this was the direction I wanted to go! But where do I start?

Naturally, I would have gone to my grandparents and asked them how they did it and copied it step by step. Unfortunately, both of my grandparents had passed away by that time. So, I took the next step, I purchased books on the subject of real estate. I read book after book after book. Then watched YouTube video after YouTube video on how to build wealth in real estate. I submerged myself in the real estate markets daily, sometimes staying up after I put my kids to bed, until 3am to learn more and more.

After about 6 months of daily learning, I had saved up enough money to purchase my first multi-unit rental property. I was extremely nervous and had many people tell me don't do it! I find it so amazing that people who have not invested in real estate say you will lose money in it! Some people have a problem for every solution in life! I quickly learned that I need to listen to the people who are successful in the field I am entering. People are naturally scared to lose money, so they gave me advice that is "safe". "Don't invest, you can lose your money." "You will lose everything if the market crashes". The list goes on and on. Keep in mind they said all of this before even hearing what deal I found to invest in! I learned I must keep a tight circle of influence around me. This circle had to consist of people who are successful at what I want to do. Luckily, I had some friends who invested in real estate and helped me make the right decision by moving forward with my first multi-unit rental property. This changed my life forever.

Now that I had my first multi-unit rental property, I reinvested the monthly passive cash flow into multiple other types of businesses. I reinvested in a retail store, a local supermarket, t-shirt company, and TV provider company. The reality is, not all of those businesses were huge successes but they did make money and continued to build my knowledge and asset column. Soon, that one multi-unit rental property funded multiple streams of income to the point where I had enough to purchase my first apartment complex. That's right! I achieved a big bucket list item by allowing my money to make more money! My cash flow continues to multiply because first I invested, and second I lived by my 70/30 rule which I will cover later in this book.

In the next chapter, I have broken down my most impactful key lessons into 7 simple steps. As you read each step, I recommend writing down in your own words what each step means to you. This will help you mentally wrap your head around the mindset you must have to make smart decisions for your financial future.

CHAPTER TWO

1. **Make the decision that you are going to achieve financial freedom!**

   There will be many obstacles that will come in the way of you and your financial freedom. You must commit to yourself now, that you will not give in to those obstacles and you will see your project through. This at times may be difficult but not impossible!

   Be prepared to sacrifice time, money, and luxury items in life to help you get to your end goal. I can assure you the sacrifice will not go in vain if you are truly committed to seeing all 7 steps through.

   Eliminate the excuses and focus on the "how" you can make it happen!

2. **Balance your finances!**

   At the beginning of your wealth building journey it will be crucial for you to balance out your finances. What does this mean? Well, let me to tell you as simply as I can. Have enough income coming in to pay your bills and have enough left over to invest. Investing does not mean "save". Don't get me wrong, you should always make it a point to have enough money in your savings to cover any unexpected bills that may come up. However, you should also work to have enough left over for you to invest.

For example, if you work full time at a 40 hour per week job at $15 per hour, you make $600 weekly. After taxes you probably take home about $500 weekly. This comes out to $2,000 take home for the month. (4 weeks in a month). If your rent is $500 per month, utilities are $100 per month, food is $200 per month, gas is $150 per month and your "play money" is around $500 per month. Then your total expenses are $1,450. In this scenario, the extra cash you have per month is $550. Keep in mind you may have other expenses that were not mentioned in this example but the same math formula applies (Total Income – Total Expenses

= Your Investment Money). You should save that $550 each month until you reach around $5,000 in your savings (will take roughly 9 months). After you have your, what I like to call "cushion money", then you start to invest the $550 per month into assets. If you are starting out your wealth building journey with too much expenses and it is not leaving you with extra money each month to invest, then you must take one of the following two actions:

- **Earn more income per month**
  - This may include you getting a second part time job or even finding a new first job that will pay you more.
- **Reduce your expenses**
  - This may include downgrading your car to decrease the loan payments. Your asset income can pay for a new one later down the line. You can also drop your "fun" expenses such as staying home on the weekend vs going out.

Remember, you must sacrifice at the beginning to get the big reward at the end.

3. **You need to "Learn" first, then you can remove the "L" (Earn)!**

Whatever you choose as your passion to build in your asset column, you must first minimize risk by learning about that particular field. Key ways I have done this throughout the years is talking to people who are in that field. Don't be afraid to ask the tough questions. If you are shy, you can always use Google to search the field you are interested in and read multiple articles to wrap your head around the ins and outs of that field. YouTube is another great source to type your questions in and watch videos of people who have been successful in the field you want to grow in.

I have also invested in myself! Mentorship is a great way to go to add rocket fuel to your assets! Having one on one attention to help guide your decisions in the right direction helps tremendously and can pay huge returns on your small investment! It amazes me how many people will spend $100+ per weekend on drinks at a bar, but will hesitate on spending the same $100 on a mentorship class that can help make them millions.

4. TAKE ACTION!

It's crazy to me how many people have the desire to be financially free yet only talk about it. Don't be one of those people! When you are done researching your desired assets, ask yourself this one simple question, "What is the next step to starting this venture?" Whatever the answer is, don't hesitate or wait! Take action!

5. Be organized!

As your assets start to grow, it will be even more important for you to develop your organizational skills. You will have too much going on for you to remember what needs to happen daily. Make a list of what you should do daily, weekly, monthly, quarterly, and yearly and make it visible for you to see daily. This will help you stay focused on what needs to happen daily to build your assets.

I have personally set up my e-mail calendar to be my database for my daily agenda. Anytime something new comes up, I add to my calendar the time frame and a quick subject of what the reminder is for. This helps me not lose track of the activities I have throughout the day to grow my assets. If you do not have an e-mail account, I recommend setting one up immediately and start getting familiar with how the calendar section works.

6. **Continue to reinvest at least 70% of your profits! Live by the 70/30 Rule!**

As your asset column grows, I see many people make the mistake of spending everything they have. Don't do this! It is amazing how quickly your wealth multiples when you make the commitment to reinvest a minimum 70% of your asset money into the same investment or another. It is staggering how quickly this multiplies and gets you to the point of financial freedom. It will be hard at first to see money coming in and not be tempted to buy your first exotic car or large house. Always remember, only spend 30% of your asset income on luxury items. Keep reinvesting the 70% and you will be able to get that exotic car you always wanted in a short period of time.

As an example, let's say you invest your day to day income in a frozen yogurt store. Over time and with the right focus you build that income to $10,000 a month. If you spend this money on luxury expenses then you can't multiply it. But, if you live by my 70/30 rule and spend $3,000 (30%) a month on any expenses that you may want or have. The other $7,000 (70%) could be reinvested into let's say another yogurt shop. Over time this second yogurt shop should yield a similar return of $10,000 a month. Now leaving you with $6,000 a month towards expenses and $14,000 to reinvest. If you keep this process going, you can see it quickly multiples into enough asset income to be financially free!

7. Delegate!

The last and final step for you to enjoy the fruits of your labor is to delegate the day to day responsibilities of your assets to an individual. That's right, this requires you to train a responsible individual to run your day to day operation so that way you can take a step back and enjoy your life. It is important to trust the person who will oversee your assets. Live by the words trust but verify! Always verify they are doing a good job for you by frequently inspecting. It is much less time consuming to verify an asset is running efficiently, than running it yourself. Once you have fully trained this person, you can now take a big step back from your asset operation and spend much more time with your family!

CHAPTER THREE

➢ **Have the right mindset**

You must prepare for many obstacles on your journey to financial freedom. Don't be so fearful of failure that you never start your journey. Have the mindset that you are capable of taking on any task and willing to put in the work to make it successful.

➢ **Become a problem solver**

It is important through your journey that you become a good problem solver! It will be key to learn to be resourceful. Your ability to use tools like Google and YouTube to help you solve problems will be vital to your success.

An example would be, if you are starting a business that has inventory, it will be vital to your business to keep track of inventory. Now, if you don't know how to do so, this can cause a huge harm to your business. I would go talk

21

to owners of other similar businesses and ask them how they keep track of inventory. Obviously you would need to give them some details first about why you are asking. You would be surprised at how many other like-minded business people love to share information. If that seems intimidating, you can always conduct a Google search and read many different articles on how to track inventory. The key is to not allow the obstacle to stop you from being successful. Use your burning desire for success as a motivator to find the answers you need to move forward!

➤ **Don't be afraid to lose money**

I have seen so many people throughout my life say they don't want to invest because they don't want to lose money. This blows me away! You must have the mentality that first, you are investing to multiply your money (not lose it) and second, you will lose any possibility of financial freedom if you are not willing to risk anything. Aside from winning the lottery, you must be willing to invest your money into assets to have them grow to the point of allowing financial freedom to happen.

> ➢ **Minimize risk by gaining knowledge**

The best way to minimize potential loss on an investment is by fully researching the opportunity prior to investing in it. For example, if I was to invest in a plumbing company, it would be wise for me to research how much it would cost to hire plumbers and how much the marketing would be to earn the jobs to have the plumbers work. If I blindly go into the business, I may be fighting an uphill battle due to the cost of the business being more than what it generates in revenue. The best way I minimize risk is finding multiple different sources to gather my information from. I hold the most value in information provided by people who are currently doing what I want to accomplish.

➢ Seek advice from the right people

It is wise to listen to the advice of everyone. It is unwise to follow the advice of people who are not successful at the plan you are putting into action. Be careful around people who have a problem for every solution. There are many of them out there!

➢ Don't procrastinate

The #1 killer of dreams is procrastination. I have never looked at a calendar and found "someday" on it. It just doesn't exist. It is important to take action daily on the next steps of your venture! Don't wait, you are only prolonging your ability to be financially free and spending more time with your loved ones.

➢ Love the game

Imagine building wealth is like playing a game. Stay within the basic rules of wealth building and have fun! The moment it doesn't seem fun to you, don't quit! Just learn to get a full night's rest and have at it tomorrow. It is important for you to be a driven individual. Often, you will not have someone in your corner cheering you on, so self-motivation is key. Learn to rest when frustrated and not quit.

➢ **Never test the waters with both feet**

Diversifying your investments is always a good option. For example, if you have all of your investments in the stock market and the stock market drops it can hurt you significantly. It is always recommended to find a minimum of 7 sources of income so if one falls short the rest are there to continue to drive your asset income forward.

I strongly recommend keeping your day to day income producing job until your assets produce enough to cover all of your family's expenses with just 30% of your assets income. For example, your assets generate $25,000 per month in income. If your family's expenses are not larger than $7,500 per month then you now have the decision to make if you would like to keep your day to day job.

> ## A goal without a deadline is just a dream

It is important to write down your daily, weekly, monthly, quarterly, and yearly goals. These goals should always include a deadline of when you are going to complete them. Setting a committed deadline to your goal will force you to stay narrowly focused on achieving your goal. This will help you minimize the distractions and deadly procrastination.

For example: "I will create $20,000 a month in passive income through real estate by XX/XX/XXXX date".

Notice how I have a clear measureable goal? I did not set a goal for myself to be "financially free" or to be "rich". If I did, how would I know if I am now "rich"? I set a solid number of $20,000 per month so I have a clear picture of when my goal has been achieved.

- ➤ **A goal without a step by step plan is also just a dream**

  After you set a real obtainable goal and write it down, the next step is to create your step by step action plan to get there. Take the time to do your research on how other people have accomplished this similar goal and again set dates for deadlines.

  For example, if my goal is to create $20,000 a month in passive income through real estate by XX/XX/XXXX, then the following step by step action items may look like this:

  - o By XX/XX/XXXX I will learn how I can buy rental income real estate with little or no money down.
  - o By XX/XX/XXXX I need to have identified the property or properties that will get me there financially.
  - o By XX/XX/XXXX I need to have funding secured for the property or properties that I will be purchasing.

- By XX/XX/XXXX I will have closed escrow on these properties.
- By XX/XX/XXXX I will have the property manager(s) set up.

The key is to be as specific as possible on each step. Work towards these steps daily. You will be amazed at what you can accomplish over the course of a month with daily action taken towards your goal.

➢ **Don't hide your goals from yourself**

Write down your goals on a board and keep that somewhere visible every day (bedroom, office, living room, or kitchen). You will use this as your daily reminder to work on your big vision goals.

Write down your daily action item goals each morning on paper and don't procrastinate! Learn to knock them out quickly! Creating this checklist daily will keep you on track to your goals. Small improvements each day will deliver HUGE improvements to your wealth over time!

> ## Stay Positive

Stay focused on being positive. It is tough to do considering how most of what you see on TV shows, news, and movies are focused on negative events or gossip. Stay focused on positive things and life will always pull through with positive things happening. It works like clockwork! Over time you will begin to live a happier life in general because you will not get frustrated with the small stuff. Stay happy my friends!

> ## Be confident

I used to look at people like Bill Gates, Steve Jobs, and Jeff Bezos as people that almost seemed much more than just men. As time goes on I realized these people all have one big thing in common. They are humans and make mistakes like you and me. They just use the lessons of mistakes and failures to learn. They in turn make better decisions because of it. With that being said, be confident! You have the power to become anything you want! Truly believe that deep down inside and watch as time passes it becomes true!

> **Learn from your mistakes**

First thing you need to know is you WILL make mistakes. Second thing you need to know is that some mistakes are OK!

When I make a mistake or have a failed investment, I take it as a learning lesson. I often look back and ask myself, "What could I have done different to drive a better outcome?" This self-reflection is key to success. You can't change other people or their actions, but you sure can change your future decisions based on your "learning lessons" in life.

I once invested a significant (relative to my income at the time) amount of cash into a business that was shut down just 1 week after the doors opened. I was devastated! After many days of being frustrated I took the time to self-reflect and ask, "What could I have done different?" I quickly realized I could have done some more research on the ins and outs of that business and avoided the financial loss. However, this was actually the first retail business I had ever started. Instead of viewing it as a financial loss I changed my viewpoint. I view it as, I paid for a valuable lesson on how to negotiate a lease agreement with a commercial property manager and set up a retail business. I learned how to hire employees, create schedules, organize inventory, and keep track of sales and products. This lesson that I paid for ended up helping out my next retail business I opened and since has been doing very well.

➢ **Find your passion**

Asset building is a lot of hard work at the beginning, but should be tons of fun for you!

Find what makes you happy and turn that into a business!

For me, I personally love real estate! The thought of hundreds of families having a nice place to live because I set up the right environment brings me joy.

If you like baseball, for example, then maybe you should invest in a business of batting cages. Or set up a coaching service for baseball.

If you like acting, as another example, then perhaps you should learn how to make YouTube videos. Start producing your own videos and posting them on YouTube for a profit.

➢ **Circle of Influence**

I am a firm believer in 'you are who you hang out with'. It is important that you hang out with the right people. If you hang out with people who live with their parents and never want to better their financial situation, then most of the time you will stoop to their way of thinking. Choose your friends with likeminded mentalities and they will help you with your plans as you do with theirs. You will always be the sum of the top 5 people you hang out with. Choose your circle wisely!

➢ **It's ok to want nice things! Use that desire as motivation**

So many people told me while growing up, enjoy what you have and stop desiring the nice things other people have. Instead of giving into that, I used that desire as motivation to build my asset income in order to afford those nice things. For example, I wanted to have a large home in a great neighborhood for my family. Our first home was small and in a very rough neighborhood. I used that as motivation to invest in real estate to build enough passive income to cover the expense of moving my family into a much bigger home in an amazing neighborhood.

➢ **Sacrifice at the beginning and reap the rewards later**

When your friends want to go out and blow money out the expense column, it's ok to say no and focus on your wealth building. At first, sacrifices must be made for the benefit of a brighter future for you and your family. I'm not saying don't go out and have fun. I'm explaining that at the beginning it is not wise to blow your money on "luxuries". It is wise to use that extra $100 you have on your business, to turn it into much more as time goes on.

➢ **Learn to prioritize**

Everyone can think of a million things to do every day. Start each day by writing down what you need to do, then write down what you want to do. Start with your "need" to do column then get to the "want" to do list. Most people start with their want to do list and never

make it a priority to get to the need to do
items.

CONCLUSION

In conclusion, I wrote this book to be as simple, short, and straight forward as possible! You have made an important and wise step by purchasing and reading this book. Now, follow the steps and don't allow anything to get in the way. There will be many obstacles that will come in the way. Learn to steer away from them and stay focused on your 7 step journey. It may take a month, a year, or even a few years to get through all 7 steps. I can assure you, your future self will thank you for sticking to it! It will not be a "piece of cake" journey, but as you get better at the game through hard work and perseverance, it pays off for generations! Thank you again for reading this book and God bless you on your journey!

\-   Michael A. Hatfield

If you would like one on one help with going through each of the steps, I offer a personal mentorship service. This service includes conference calls and/or facetime discussions to help you make smart wealth building decisions. Cheers to your financial freedom journey!

For more information regarding my one on one mentoring service please e-mail StopComplainingandGetRich@outlook.com

If you have purchased this book on Amazon you will receive an additional 20% off my one on one mentorship program